Mai
is the name of a flower

WOMEN LOVED BY THE VETERANS OF VIET-NAM

By
Erik Robertssen

Edited By
Daniel Brick

The Anvil Press

Library of Congress Catalog Card Number: 78-56936
International Standard Book Number: 0-918552-03-6

The Husbandman first appeared as *Soldier* in the **Smith Park Poetry Series Broadside Collection,** 1975.

Air Cambodia Stewardess first appeared in **The North Country Anvil,** Number 7, August-September, 1973.

Flight of the C-5 first appeared as *C-5, A Eulogy for Margaret Moses* in **The North Country Anvil,** Number 15, August-September, 1975.

P.O.W. (Returned) Wife first appeared in **Demilitarized Zones, Veterans After Vietnam,** East River Anthology, 1976.

Mai is the Name of a Flower first appeared as *In Viet Nam Mai is the Name of a Flower* in **The North Country Anvil,** Number 8, October-November, 1973.

Published By

The Anvil Press

Millville, Minnesota 55957

Printed in The United States of America

How can I have been so full of her
he thought
and so empty now?
All the joy
can it be gone with her
and nothing remain?

To keep.
To preserve.
To feel her touch
ever soft
ever warm
ever fresh.

Alone in the dark
hollow in the silence
this he resolved:

to build for her
a Taj Mahal of words
and so
to live her
again.

WOMEN LOVED BY THE VETERANS OF VIET-NAM

-contents-

Huong   *Lullaby of the Rockets*

Colette-Xuan   *The Husbandman*

Young Woman, Unknown   *Air Cambodia Stewardess*

Bach-Thuy   *The Debacle*

Margaret   *Flight of the C-5*

Infant Girl, Unknown   *The 105 Millimeter Vase*

Nancy-Thu   *My Trip to the Mountains*

Nguyet   *The Daughter of No One*

Quyen-Nhu   *Saigon Daughter*

Caroline   *Rich Lady*

Tuyet-Hoa   *Tangerine*

Minh-Duc   *Clerk in a Fancy Souvenir Shop*

Carmen   *Carmen, Who Makes Photographs*

Celina   *Coming Home*

Jane   *Lawyer's Wife*

Ellen   *M.I.A. Wife*

Ingrid   *P.O.W. (Returned) Wife*

Rina   *Rina, World and Time*

Margie   *Visit to the Swedish Church*

Ngoc-Mai   *Soldier's Girl, Night I*

Soldier's Girl, Night II

Mai is the Name of a Flower

Mai

is the name of a flower

Huong

(Rose)

Viet-Nam

Lullaby of the Rockets

In Viet Nam nights
lovers
and all others
falling asleep together
never say
good night.
They always say
good-bye.

Colette - Xuan

(Colette-Springtime)

Viet-Nam

The Husbandman

I. 1968

Suddenly
they were swept apart by the fighting.
For seventeen days
neither knows
whether the other
is alive
or dead.

Months before
he had taken her.
Not to love.
Only to have.
Then he would not hurt
when he left her world for his.

Now
the bodies make him know it will hurt:
bodies on the road, crushed by tanks
bodies in houses, slumped over tables
bodies in ditches, a frozen hand reaching
bodies in the grass, green thick with black
bodies in heaps, burned to the bone
a woman, her legs wide apart.

In the burning yellow days
his eyes sweeping the tree line
horizon smoking, rumbling
he can push her from his thoughts.

In the heavy black nights
huddled behind sandbags
orange slashing, silver blinding
he cannot hold her back.

At daybreak
hot gold rays reaching into black
draw up the thick grey dew
glistening on the blackened bodies
and fire a swirling violet mist
sweet and sick with a shocking perfume:
the essence of the dead distilled.

Sitting, staring
swept in the sweet wet violet
his lungs fill with the bodies
and the red in his veins streams to purple
searing rivers
rushing a scalding message of humanity
to flood every cell.
He is on fire
everywhere
with their pain.

He doubles forward
clutching his chest
his body aching
to make a child
his logic says resist.

II. 1973

Late November field in the silence of sunset
dry brown grass stiff with frost
he rides the back of the little orange tractor
bucking
engine whining
rising and falling over the furrows
a small boat beneath a vast sky.

Deerhide collar up
wide-brimmed hat tipped low over his eyes
purple, red and blue of the horizon
light his face golden
and his narrowed eyes gleam phosphorescent
with the secret of the cold black dirt:
pregnant.

Young Woman

(Unknown)

Cambodia

Air Cambodia Stewardess
at the
Phnom Penh Airport

Struggling to preserve gentility
in the midst of war
you stand on the broken concrete runway
at the door of the miniature terminal
greeting passengers.

Tall for your people
slender
slight
wrapped in a long straight skirt
deep green
that skims the ground
a flowing green scarf around your neck
fatigue rounds your shoulders
and bends your head forward.

Too exhausted to speak
you nod gravely at each arrival.

Above your head

a corner of the tower ripped away by a rocket

fighter-bombers screaming

helicopter gunships beating the air

and two kilometers away

the green earth strewn with craters.

Your eyes cast downward

you think perhaps we cannot see.

But I can see.

I know Asian eyes now

and I can see

the fatigue

and behind that

the fear.

It's time now for you to decide.

For you

Bangkok is an hour and a half away.

Young woman of this wet green country

so full of life

and death

please live.

Go. Fly. Disappear.

Go, please

and live.

I want to see your children.

Bach-Thuy

(Crystal Water)

Viet-Nam

The Debacle

Her conical straw hat still rests on my bookshelf.
If you hold it against the light
you can read on the underside
an old and lovely poem about Hue.
Her bright blue ao-dai
sheer and silken
and swept over with tiny orange flowers
still hangs in my closet.
Her pale pink lipstick
fresh and perfumed at early morning partings
is still sweet and cool on my lips
but I let her go.

There would always be time, we agreed.
She would be sure to get out before.
So I watched her jet
race down the snow-edged runway
and heard the engines crack the ice-crystalled air.

She had cried in her sleep the night before
turning and turning
and I begged her
not to go.

But
black eyes flashing anger
watching pictures in her head
she said there were children to get out first
silent babies
in large dark rooms
flat in iron-barred cribs
staring.

"The innocents," she said bitterly
tossing her head, her hair flying
"and the government does nothing."

Of course there would be time
months probably
weeks and weeks at least
and I would come
to bring her out.

But

overnight

too fast to be believed

headlines grow tall and black like tombstones

blood runs red from my television

and yellow bodies fall twitching

and there is nothing left of us

but broken words

shouted between waves of static

across the Pacific

and cables

frantic

cryptic in love and fear:

"Come!   Instantly!   Love...."

"Can't!   Government won't permit!

Don't forget!   Forever.....Forever....."

And she

harried among rows of cribs

reaching at once

for diapers, bottles, needles, mosquito netting

brushing flies from damp foreheads

probably will not even hear them

when they come for her.

Margaret

Australia

Flight of the C-5
A   Eulogy

Margaret

gentle Margaret

I didn't think it would be you.

You

in the crumbling villa

always the softest

hushed

among the babies wailing

the staff shouting

in the heat

and flies

and dripping diapers

and fear.

You never cared to be called

Angel of the Battlefield Orphanages

and against would-be parents

half crazy with child possession

shrieking ten thousand miles by telephone

you never raised your voice

sweetly disarming

in melodic Australian.

You never cared to be called Saviour
but saviour you were
damp hair clinging to your forehead
the same dress for days
until you remembered to change
padding about softly in bare feet
shoulders sagging
but never stopping.

And so cool
you seemed to walk above the others
in misty mountains.
It would have surprised most to see you
collapsed on the sofa
a bottle of scotch in your arm
a quart, I think it was
and on your phonograph
the same Chopin playing and playing and playing.
After all
the boy
was only one of many children
twelve that week, if I remember
to be laid out
stiff
in a cardboard box.

In those times

it was my comfort to imagine you in future years

back in your own country

aging

and grown-up children

almond-eyed

taller than they would have been in their country

coming to your door with flowers.

And you would have only smiled.

No, Margaret

I didn't think it would be you in the screaming

cartwheeling in the air among pieces of children

smashed and torn and burning

as the flaming giant

slams

into the earth.

And they never even found

your body

Angel.

Infant Girl

(Unknown)

Viet-Nam

The One Hundred Five Millimeter Vase

Gleaming

graceful

golden.

Inward

outward

upward flowing

once brought forth death, destruction

how fitting now it serves a coffin.

Hammered molten

shaped and polished

now entombs a dream demolished.

Those on whom it once rained terror

fought to overcome the horror

and from it beauty wrought.

Strange things happen in war:
against death
the wit employs art to create.
Stranger still more
how witless cells
with their own secret art
draw together to overcome their fate.

In the fear and in the dying
shock
sweeps a man and woman together:
a wanting deep beyond knowing
creates a child
to make forever.

But in war ironies mount unending:
now their altar holds the vase
with cold black ashes 'til eternity bearing.
Inside
a child rests
in brass and space.

Nancy-Thu

(Nancy Autumn)

Viet-Nam

My Trip to the Mountains and the Seashore

by

Nancy-Thu

Age 9

My father, you know, he American

and he don't want me

and my mother, you know, she sick

sick sick sick

and my mother she die

and she give my sister money

and she say my sister

take me Da-Lat

and my mother she die

and my sister she take me Da-Lat

and I go look look look

and we go Nha-Trang

and I look look look

everywhere I look look

and then we don't have money

and my sister

she take me home.

Nguyet

(Moon)

Viet-Nam

The Daughter of No One

Ten
a little old to be adopted
she stands off to the side
out of the picture
but not quite out of the picture
her eyes half lowered.

Him
only three
being held for the picture
she knows is a sign
soon he will be gone.

He will go to The Land Of The Beautiful.
To those who will have the picture
he will be a son.

And she

of the red hair

and green eyes slanting

abandoned

among the black hair

and brown eyes slanting

silently

in her tiny heart

hoping

"If they see me in the picture...."

Quyen – Nhu

(Songbird)

Viet-Nam

Saigon Daughter

Heat
voices rising, falling

air
    wet and grey, spiced and sick with charcoal smoke
hanging

water
    in ditches, still with oil and slime, green
thickening

shacks
    with walls of flattened beer cans, grey tin roofs
    half orange
rusting

flags
    once yellow and red scorched white and brown
    stiff
crumbling

girls
    walking mud rutted roads, high black shoes
    golden silk
floating

Quyen-Nhu
I want
you.

Heat
voices rising, falling

skies
    particled in brown, sun-fired dust clouds
sweeping

wires
    from tipped, broken-sparred telephone poles
    twisted, frayed
sagging

garbage
    scattered over streets of broken concrete
    smashed grapefruit, torn gardenias
baking

fish
    laid in the dust to dry, fly-covered
    eyes gone, brown, curled
parching

girls
    on motor bicycles in clouds of blue
    white-gloved hands, long black hair
flying

Quyen-Nhu
I want
you.

Heat
voices rising, falling

signs
    with street names on building corners
    jagged with bullet punctures, bent, chipped
peeling

bunkers
    low behind limp barbed wire, rotted sandbags
spilling

temples
    with needle spires shrouded in ash, walls
    soaked in incense, mildew, grey vaulted chambers
looming

coffins
    gleaming amber in stacks and stacks
    honey-coated in lacquer syrup, open
inviting

girls
    in flower gardens raising tall, smeared glasses
    bottomless black eyes in almond corners
    pink-frosted mouths curving
drinking
thick, clear liquid
sweet, sweet, sweet and choking
crushed jasmine petals and sugar.

Quyen-Nhu
I want
you.

Heat
voices murmuring, murmuring

breezes
    through night of damp black cotton
    soft, cool
caressing

lanterns
    from behind shutters of silent white houses
    dim, yellow
flickering

arms
    bare in gentle golden light
    warm, perfumed
waiting

silver flash!
    walls crashing
                    plaster pouring
                            blue-glowing steel
slicing

girls
    on white sheets drenched in red
screaming
reaching

Quyen-Nhu
daughter of my fear
I want you.

Caroline

United States

Rich Lady

There is an edge in her voice   of ice

an unbending in her carriage   of steel

a hardness in her touch   of marble

an unchanging in her color   of ivory

a bitterness in her perfume   of cloves

an unyielding in her embrace   of death

but a depth in her eyes   of infinity

Her eyes

draw in souls

and

all else

lies.

Her eyes

draw in souls

until

she cries.

And then

she is

ice

steel

marble

ivory

cloves

and

death.

And

she

survives.

Tuyet - Hoa

(Snow Flower)

Viet-Nam

Tangerine

Tangerine is in the sky!

Tangerine is the sun exploding!

Tangerine is colors!

hair	raven, sable, mahogany, chestnut
eyes	violet, plum, burgundy, cocoa
teeth	snow, pearl, alabaster, cloud
mouth	claret, cranberry, port, ruby
neck	citron, saffron, apricot, peach
arms	honey, butterscotch, carmel, mango
breasts	cream, cinnamon, coral, raspberry
hips	maize, flax, champagne, rose
legs	amber, tamarind, bronze, gold.

Tangerine is

high

and

above

and burning silent

alone

in an ice sky

and

Tangerine

has men and men and men and men and men

and men and men and men and men and men

and

Tangerine

is burning silent

alone

in an ice sky

and

Tangerine is

lemon wrists

running

cherry.

Minh - Duc

(Virtue)

Viet-Nam

Clerk in a Fancy Souvenir Shop, Vung Tau

Small

lean

hard

flat

and very taut

walking very fast

in severely cut glacier-white suit

like a dagger of ice

she sears through the blinding heat

sun rays bouncing off her

freezing into icicles pink and orange

and shattering on the sidewalk around her.

She is on her way to the shop

to make money.

Slicing in off the street
she goes to a room in the back
to change clothes next to open cans of trash.
Rising long lean arms
she showers lush black silk
extravagant with lurid pink flowers
over lean sharp shoulders
and hard flat hips
and undulating petals of rose
give her
shape
contour
flow.

She goes to the mirror
breathes deeply
and watches her face.
Under pale saffron skin
stretched translucent
over high hard cheekbones
dark shadows flicker
outlining
the small sharp skull
of a panther.

Far back
in each blackened eye hole
glimmers
a black flame.

Lean long fingers
work quickly
masking
black shadows of bone
with heavy ivory cream
and the skull
disappears
under rich creamed skin.

Thin hard lips
stretched wide
over small sharp teeth
are lacquered dewy rose
and over heavy black hair
she sprinkles an essence
of yellow gardenias
and jungle rain.

Soft

scented

seductive

she glides among rows of blue porcelain

straw flowers

silver and brass

ready to charm customers

and they would never know

looking in her face

she abandoned her baby in the jungle

to fool a man

to bring her to America

as his wife.

But as she smiles

she is always watching

her reflection in the window

and sometimes

when she is tired

she catches her breath

rushes to the room in the back

and goes to lie down

until her skull goes away.

Carmen

United States

Carmen, Who Makes Photographs

Bittersweet

she speaks little

her words cautious

quiet

tentative

but she is burning

she hangs her heart on the wall

and we see her

haunting

flaming

loving

fearing

melancholy

solitary

and we see her world

our world

bittersweet.

Celina

United States

Coming Home

Her eyes
sometimes
watchfully
she would permit him
to see them undefended
fleeting glances luminous with her pain.

Quiet converstations
late in the night
softly
slowly
small stories:

Her mother aging and alone
a ring from her divorced father
with her name spelled wrong
the suicide of a friend
a lover demanding a "dynamite personality"

Quiet conversations

late in the night

small, strong hands

fumbling

reaching

tugging gently

drawing him into the beauty of her pain.

Her fine brown hair cascading

swirling

wrapping him tenderly

a silken curtain round them both

and he is dazed in the flash of her dynamite.

Jane

United States

Lawyer's Wife, Age 36, Without Child

He
red and white striped tie
brown tweed vest
loved his name.
It was very old.

She
crystal hands
raven hair
could not make it older.

And so
each year
trembling lips flame redder
glistening eyes are edged blacker
and the yellow smoke of her cigarette
she draws
to the bottom
of her lungs.

Ellen

United States

M.I.A. Wife

Fundamentally, I suppose
she still looks the same
six years beyond her husband.
He'd be sure to recognize her.

Oh, there is some grey, of course
and the shoulders are slightly stooped
but then maybe
she's hiding from temptation.
After all
it has been a long time
no matter how much you loved.

But, don't you think the hands
are a little rougher, dryer
and don't they look, well, larger?

And there is a tendency for the nose
to redden
quite quickly
and the eyelids too.

I couldn't help thinking
her eyelids
how much better they'd look
enamelled in jade.

Better
but for
that tiny swollen blood vessel
fixed
like an angry red sucker
to the edge of a dull grey iris.
Curious
how you can tell
the eye was once
a
soft
brown.

But really
all in all
it's nothing a nice shot of hormones
estrogen
wouldn't fix up.

Hormones

yes

that's the ticket

because

it just seems that

somehow

since he went down

her juices have dried up.

Ingrid

Norway

P. O. W. (Returned) Wife

Stories
told and retold.

Someone asks him
her eyes narrow
and she looks
far
away.

He talks
and she is seeing.

In the jungle
in his terror and excitement
he never sees her.

Each story
a hundred times heard
she follows.

Each word
slashes her heart
and her smile flashes.

Her eyes shining
she nods
reaches for his hand
softly exclaims
joins his bitter laughter
and
as he gropes
shaking
for a detail lost
she reminds him.

Rina

Philippines

Rina, World and Time

I.

She took me to see a volcano.
Here it is morning, far across the Pacific
and I will know her for one day only.

Without words
she leads me across a field of rolling green
a bright floating flower
in flowing orange with brilliant yellow parasol
to where the land drops off into space
and the cool blue sky flies up and sweeps over us.

Out, over the edge
beyond the precipice
she holds out to me
an immense new world
stretching out beyond the eye
and the dilemma of the time that is here.

Down and down
far below
silent in a vast glittering lake
the green mountain broods
and all around
hills roll away
and away
and up into towering clouds.

The wind mourns, ruffling her hair.
At last she speaks, but only of the view
sighing with the wind
and she who gives her life to heal
is a mystery
of lingering pain.

At lunch in a little park
pineapple with salt
coconut milk
fish and bread
we sit among others who chatter brightly
and talk
quietly:

first

of children and disease

and then

of doctors

and then

of poets

and finally

with the sky deepening from blue to purple

of the doctor-poet Zhivago

and at last I say

"One such as you

woman

doctor

must have left a lover

to return to these islands,"

but she does not say

and I try to look

into her eyes

but she does not let me look.

II.

She took me to see her hospital.
Here it is night, far across the Pacific
and I will know her for hours only.

Without words
she leads me
past eyes of frightened parents huddling
a tiny strong ship in white
with girls in grey fluttering behind
to where a bleak dim corridor
disappears into the night.

Down, into the grey
behind rows of closed doors
she holds out to me
an immense screaming world
stretching out beyond the mind
and the dilemma of the time that is here.

Deep into the night I follow
waiting silent outside
door after door
until
her steps slower and slower
at last I say
"For this
you must require love,"
but she does not say
and I try to look
into her eyes
but she does not let me look.
Until
finally
with night-black windows edged in rose
and no time
or world
for us
she stops against a door
her hands clenched
and turns to me.

Slowly pulling back her hair
her eyes
she opens them to me
wider
and
wider.

Margie

United States

Visit to the Swedish Church and Cemetery
Spring Garden, Minnesota

Daughter of wagon-box maker, blacksmith, farmer

in bitter depression winters

in rough, handmade cutter with horse

heedless in youth and health

you pitched

and tossed

and laughed over these fields and roads

snow-drifted, ice-rutted

and now

in pain

in lush, rich green of summer come too soon

they take you back on smooth highways

nearly flying

through green sea of waving corn

to grassy island of church and graveyard

A.D. 1876

to pray

beneath towering white spire

over the graves of your parents.

Silent cemetery
under cool bright blue and brilliant orange
only whispering leaves of corn
bending, rushing, receding, lapping at its banks
and crumbling granite markers.

Stepping slowly
carefully
slowly
your face fixed to deny
white-hot lightning in your limbs
you move gently
over those who sleep not far below
and feel instead the pain
of tiny flat stones
everywhere scattered
like oats windblown
inscribed only
"Baby"
"Baby"
"Baby"
"Baby".

With two daughters trailing

lush, too

and in their time, already, of ripeness

and husband, greying, somber

you kneel in soft green grass

over mother, father

and as you say ancient words

I wonder

if you see yourself beside them soon

looking up

at your own daughters.

And to you

it seems not long ago now:

mother, father, church, school

not nearly long enough

and from those days

the future

races

brutally

into the NOW.

And I

helpless

in the time that was left

all I could do

was lead you to talk of the old times

re-live childhood days

and play for you

old immigrant songs of your father

so it would seem

though it were not true

that your life

had been

much

longer.

Ngoc – Mai

(Precious New Year's Blossom)

Viet-Nam

Soldier's Girl

Night I.

Four o'clock in the morning
alone in the bedroom hushed, still, grey
his vacant eyes fix on the ceiling:

Ten thousand miles through the night
two thousand days back through time
inside the crumbled walls of her tiny white house
he gropes for her small broken form.

Four o'clock in the morning
at the far end of the hall
faint light of the moon through the window
silver edges the doorway of the den:

Inside
in the soft velvet blackness
is someone standing?

Soldier's Girl

Night II.

All the long howling night he lies
empty vial beside his bed
still, unmoving
the poison carrying him away
farther and farther.
His blood now only trickling
and his ears not hearing
a bitter wind wailing
dry leaves tumbling
and against his window
bare black branches clawing.

All the long howling night he lies
his heart colder and colder
until
somewhere
deep
deep
deep in his unhearing ears
sobbing
she awakens him with her tears.

Trembling
he feels the sheets damp in her place
but she has been dead six years.

Mai is the Name of a Flower

In Viet Nam

Mai is the name of a flower.

Small, yellow, fragile

it blooms only at the New Year

and fades quickly.

In Viet Nam

Mai is also the name of a girl.

I came back to your country, Mai

to look for your grave

five years

after we flew you out of our surrounded camp

to a place I do not know.

Forgive us.

We didn't mean

to prevent you from being buried at your home.

You see, we hoped you would live

and no one would believe it

when the Sergeant said you had already died.

I couldn't look.

I came back to find your grave, Mai
and move it to the place
where your home had been.
The home I had to destroy.

The monk at the Buddhist cemetery at Thu Duc
(someone told us you might be there
a quiet, rambling collection of whitewashed tombs
clinging to the top of a low hill)
wanted to be helpful to the somber ex-soldier.

"Yes," he said, as he offered us tea with ice
"I seem to remember a girl the name of Mai
was brought here at the New Year of 1968."

My heart felt afraid.

He led us around the outside of the temple
six or seven small children following
whispering to each other.
We stopped in a moment
and they grew hushed.

I looked

but

the tomb was large

and covered by a portico with vines.

"No,"

it said to us

"This is not the tomb

of a poor young girl from the country."

The name belonged to someone else.

"Ah well, then,"

sighed the monk

"I must have been wrong.

There were so many then."

He smiled lamely.

We turned to go.

Mai

our moments

in the months before the madness of the New Year

were so full of promise.

I never thought the war would come to you.
How could I have known
they would be the only moments
we would have for all time?

By the first anniversary of your death
I had written a chronicle
of each of our moments.
When I wrote it
each moment was real.
Now
as I read it
for the hundredth time
I cannot be sure.

Was that Mai?
Was that what we said?
Was that just how she looked
in her yellow dress
with the yellow flowers in her hair?

Precious to me then
now I hunger after them.

I've tried so hard to preserve those moments
but Mai
in the very act
I'm losing you more.

In the time and space and life that has passed
you are slipping
slipping
the precious little details are blurring
and I have brought you back in memory
so many times
so many
many times
that I cannot feel
you
any more.
Only the memory
of a memory.

I could not find your grave, Mai
but in the place where your home had been
I found your picture.

Now I have it everywhere around me
even the room upstairs
for the little girl I hoped would come someday
and have your name.
And I carry it with me.
But
I look at your picture
and I cannot feel
you
any more.
Only the memory
of a memory.
And you are slipping
slipping
And I am helpless.

If only I could have found your grave
I could have had
at least
your coffin.
How that must seem a morbid thought.
But it would be something
something.

Mai, in your picture
you are so incredibly young and fresh
and I am growing so old.
There were only eight years between us then.
Now, can you believe it
we are eighteen years apart.
Last month I let my beard grow
and it came out all grey and white.
It was a shock.
And there are small lines now around the eyes.

Now
growing old
in a still, empty house
my only hope for us
is my death.

But Mai
when I come to you
I may be
so
old.

Will you still want me?

Typography: Jerome Braun
Printing: Jack Miller
Eric Steinmetz
Ld Albin

Cover Concept: Armi Nelson
Cover Layout: Jerome Braun
Photograph of Ngoc-Mai: Nguyen Ky, Saigon, 1968
Ngoc-Mai's Ao-Dai: Derk Hansen